MW01713723

LETTERS FROM MRS. GRUNDY

Oneita Jackson

DAKOTA AVENUE WEST Publishing

Dakota Avenue West Publishing

Detroit, Michigan

www.dakotavenuewest.com

Copyright © 2017 by Oneita Jackson

All rights reserved.

ISBN: 978-0-9986479-0-6

No part of this book may be reproduced, performed, recorded, or otherwise transmitted without written consent from Oneita Jackson, except brief quotations for critical analysis, articles, or reviews.

Back cover photo by Regina H. Boone.

Design by Shon Norman of SoundThought Graphics.

Hair by Lizzy Chamberlain of Edwin Paul Salon, Grosse Pointe Woods, Michigan.

Nails by Anita Sewell.

Handwriting by Oneita Jackson.

Alex Cruden, editor

Printed and published in the United States by Dakota Avenue West Publishing, LLC.

Also by Oneita Jackson

Nappy-Headed Negro Syndrome

Acclaim for *Nappy-Headed Negro Syndrome*

"Damned funny, scalpel-sharp, and moves like a rocket." DAVE EGGERS

Acclaim for *Letters from Mrs. Grundy*

"This is trademark Oneita Jackson, wherein she destroys all worldly pretense with wit and never wastes a word. This time, in brief notes to unsuspecting clerks and other interpersonal gatekeepers, she puts into words the daily devastation we feel when, for example, we get on a bus, smiling, and the driver upbraids us about standing in the wrong place. Jackson is funny—she is always funny—but behind the humor is a plaintive cry for humans to be humans, to be more careful and more kind."
DAVE EGGERS, international bestseller

"If you want to know what not *to do when giving service to customers, read this book! And if you want confirmation that you're not the only customer who's been asked awful questions or challenged about your choices, you'll smile and shake your head as you read. Oneita gives you straight talk and terrific insight with every anecdote—every story is sure to set you thinking."*
ARI WEINZWEIG, Zingerman's owner

"Oneita Jackson reminds us that grace, civility, and poise are still of import in the 21st Century."
JAMES DEVORE CARTER II, grandson of Ophelia DeVore, who founded the Grace del Marco modeling agency and a charm school in New York City in the 1940s

"Oneita Jackson's Letters from Mrs. Grundy *is relentlessly funny, smart and kind in the best possible way—like the author herself."* **TRACIE MCMILLAN**, New York Times bestseller and James Beard Award winner

Letters from Mrs. Grundy

is dedicated to

people who provide extraordinary service.

Letters from Mrs. Grundy

is a

work of nonfiction.

It is based on the observations
of Oneita Jackson.

Names have been changed because

this

is a

creative work of nonfiction.

GPS coordinates have been provided
because it is fun.

If you have ever let me invade your space with my stories,

if you have ever shared your heart,

shown me kindness,

THANK YOU.

Mrs. Grundy

Mrs. Grundy \mi-səz-ˈgrən-dē\ *n* : one marked by prudish conventionality in personal conduct

"Bob is a regular **Mrs. Grundy**," said Harriet, "and you'll never have any fun if you waste too much time worrying about what he thinks is proper."

DID YOU KNOW?

"What would Mrs. Grundy say?" Dame Ashfield, a character in Thomas Morton's 1798 play, *Speed the Plough*, was forever asking that question and constantly worried about invoking the sneering condemnation of her prudish neighbor Mrs. Grundy. Although that tyrant of social opinion never actually appeared on stage during the play, Mrs. Grundy's critical attitude (or fear of it) exerted a significant influence on the actions of other characters and ultimately on our language. By 1813, English-speakers had adopted her name as a byword for anyone with extremely rigid standards of propriety that he or she applied in judging (often disapprovingly) the actions of others.

WORD-A-DAY CALENDAR, March 26, 2001

Introduction

The thought of what America would be like
If the Classics had a wide circulation
    Troubles my sleep,
The thought of what America,
The thought of what America,
The thought of what America would be like
If the Classics had a wide circulation
    Troubles my sleep.
Nunc dimittis, now lettest thou thy servant,
Now lettest thou thy servant
    Depart in peace.
The thought of what America,
The thought of what America,
The thought of what America would be like
If the Classics had a wide circulation...
    Oh well!
    It troubles my sleep.

Ezra Pound

Cantico del Sole

(From *Instigations*, 1920)

[from *Pound: Poems Translations*, ed. Richard Sieburth, Library of America, 2003]

Now as we know, there are few things more dangerous than remedies. When I was a teen, I went on dates to the pool at Anacostia. I was in love with Pound's *Cantos*, but it was only later that I found that Pound was incarcerated at the St. Elizabeth's madhouse and picnicked with his friends along the Potomac River in Anacostia. I have a fantasy that I might have seen the Poundians at some point, sitting in the grass and raging against all of the failures of American civilization. It's a sort of new version of "six degrees of separation." But in this version of the game, there is no dividing line at all between knowing the truth and being crazy. Salvador Dali said it best: "The only difference between me and a madman is that I'm not mad." But all of this has been willfully forgotten.

Also included in the forgotten is the wonderful production of an insect poet jumping up and down on typewriter keys. "I will write you a series of poems/showing how things look/to a cockroach" says Don Marquis's Archy. The first *Archy and Mehitabel* came out in 1927 and has never been out of print. But I think the disapproval has been glossed over. The book is read as merely something that is cute. The animal characters perhaps defray some of the problems of presenting a dispenser of disapproval.

When respectability was a driving force in society, Mrs. Grundy conveyed that there was something to the idea that attention must be paid to what one is doing. Now a new Mrs. Grundy has been erected in the 21st Century by Oneita Jackson, and she comes from her troubled sleep to put some stick about. There are going to be some consequences to the general dishevelment of the quotidian order. She is opposed to chaos, laxity, sloth, fakery, and bewilderment. If you get a whack, just assume that you deserved it. Don't try to take Mrs. Grundy down for your own comfort. Try to own up to your deficiencies.

It's good for civilization.

JON WOODSON, author of *Endowed, a comic novel* and *Summer Games*

"You are a server's worst nightmare."

SYLVIA RECTOR, to Oneita, during a conversation about yet another unpleasant dining experience. Rector was the Detroit Free Press restaurant critic, and during the 11 years Oneita worked as a copy editor at the newspaper, she regaled the newsroom with tales, reserving the most delicious ones for Sylvia.

"You sound like Jack Nicholson in Five Easy Pieces, *O."*

MARTHA THIERRY, a graphics editor, after she heard Oneita ordering vegetables from the Doubletree hotel next door to the Free Press. Oneita had heard of, but had never seen, the infamous Chicken Salad Sandwich scene from the 1970 movie, so she and Martha watched it together on the copy desk. When Oneita was a cab driver, she drove comedian J. Anthony Brown to a radio station at 5:00 a.m. and offered to get him breakfast. His order was specific: chicken breast, plain; egg whites, no salt; toast, no butter. Unlike Lorna Thayer in the movie, the waitress at Plakas in Greektown was accommodating and helpful: She kept offering more food for less money. "I appreciate your help, but I need you to put this order in *exactly* the way I'm asking for it," Oneita said. Then she asked the waitress,

"Have you seen *Five Easy Pieces*? Well, put the order in and I'll pull it up on my phone. You are going to crack up."

"You are a bitch."

PAULETTE MITCHELL, No. 11 Friend, almost daily. (Oneita has 10 Best Friends.)

"You have range."

ALEX CRUDEN, Oneita's editor, who wastes no words, responding to Paulette's observation, as Oneita pouted during lunch at La Feria in Midtown.

Dear Reader,

When I was a child, my father used to tell people about my one observation during Easter. I could accept the idea that Jesus died on the cross to save our sins and that the two Marys went to the tomb and He wasn't there and that one day He was coming back for you and for me, but I could not accept this one thing about Resurrection Sunday and I always asked him: "Daddy, how can a rabbit lay a chicken egg?"

I enjoyed reading as a child, devouring my monthly subscription to Ebony Jr! and scrutinizing the Miss Manners column Sundays in the Dayton Daily News. I continued to read Judith Martin's etiquette pieces in the Washington Post during college.

When I was a concierge in Bethesda, Maryland, in 1993, we had to read Letitia Baldrige's *New Complete Guide to Executive Manners* and take a test on it. I did very well on the test. There was an extra credit part where we were asked to write about anything we wanted to from the book. I wrote about the thing that struck me most: the placement of chopsticks at the end of a meal. Seems I'd been disrespecting Chinese culture for a very long time.

Several years ago, my friends and I were

walking out of a movie theater, discussing the documentary we'd just seen, *Into Great Silence.* It is a 162-minute movie about monks who never talk. There is a delightful part where they *do* talk, though, during a ski trip in the French Alps, and they are quite funny. But the one thing that struck me as peculiar was the fact that the monk who delivered the food used a key to open each person's box. "Why does he need a key? Why is the box locked?" I said. "They're *monks.* Who's going to steal food in the monastery?" I was with a mother and daughter. The older woman said, "Well, if that's all you got out of the film, you didn't get anything." But that's what struck *me*.

In his review of *Nappy-Headed Negro Syndrome*, my former Detroit Free Press colleague Ron Bernas writes: "Oneita started as a copy editor and not long afterward was sharing her skills and insights in all sorts of ways, culminating in a regular column about life in Detroit as seen by an out-of-towner. She looked at the region's idiosyncrasies with a raised eyebrow that asked, 'What the hell?' and left us natives hard-pressed to explain them." That's the standard: I write about things that strike me.

I had not planned to write *Letters from Mrs. Grundy*. The book started as one letter to a shop owner, but as I continued to write,

I became more infuriated as I recalled my collective distasteful experiences and out came an effusive commentary on the denialist culture of the service industry. As I was completing this book, my editor, Alex, asked two poignant questions: "Do you think they were doing it knowingly or unknowingly?" and "Are they being put down because of their ignorance or thoughtlessness?"

I told him I thought they were doing it unknowingly and they were being put down because it should be someone's responsibility to make sure they were not ignorant or thoughtless, that someone should be in charge of expediting the happiness. This book isn't about me: I am writing on behalf of people who are routinely offended and insulted by customer service professionals, and as an Art Buchwald- and Ambrose Bierce-loving satirist, I take my work seriously. "Satire is malicious," Buchwald said in *Malice on Purpose*. "It is a way to express an opinion and also make the reader laugh."

If the tone of this book strikes you as harsh, it should. Satire is "a malicious business, but someone has to do it," Buchwald wrote. My ink pen allows me a freedom my home training does not, though sometimes I act like I have no home training, at all. Strict. Upbringing. My Mommy is a black woman from Birmingham,

Alabama. Her mother was a black woman from Birmingham, Alabama. Baptist-church-going women with impeccable manners.

There was no escaping matters of propriety. I had a Militant Manners Maven at home; she had soldiers at school. Everyone in Dayton Public Schools, from the principal to the janitor, seemed to be invested in our academic and social intelligence. There is an entire section on my grade-school report cards that measures Personal and Social Growth in three areas: Healthful Living, Personal Development, Work Habits and Attitudes. S—Good Progress. I—Needs to Improve. U—Unsatisfactory. A checkmark meant we needed to improve.

We were monitored each quarter in eight areas of Personal Development:

____ Practice correct etiquette

____ Be courteous

____ Show respect for the rights of others

____ Get along well with others

____ Respect authority

____ Show growth in self-control

____ Accept responsibility willingly

____ Accept constructive criticism

Mommy. Dayton Public Schools. Church. Mrs. Grundy cannot even stand next to me.

Ask my son.

One day we were eating at the kitchen table and I scolded him for something when he asked, "Mom, is there an etiquette for everything?" I pushed back from the table, grabbed him by his elbow, and led him to the living room, to the Etiquette Section of our library. I took his index finger, pointed at the books, and moved it across as I read the names:

Miss Manners' Guide to Excruciatingly Correct Behavior, Judith Martin

Emily Post, Laura Claridge

Prudent Advice, Jaime Morrison Curtis

Social Q's, Philip Galanes

The Official Preppy Handbook, Lisa Birnbach, ed.

How to Build a Fire, Erin Bried

The Modern Gentleman, Phineas Mollod and Jason Tesauro

Choosing Civility, P.M. Forni

Etiquette, Peggy Post

The New Emily Post's Etiquette, Elizabeth L. Post

Emily Post's The Gift of Good Manners, Peggy Post and Cindy Post Senning

An Uncommon History of Common Courtesy, Bethanne Patrick

Kids' Little Instruction Book, Jim & Steve Dodson

What to Do When No One Has a Clue, Stephanie Pierson and Barbara Harrison

How to Be a Gentleman, John Bridges

Habitus Disgusticus, Ian Whitelaw

New Rules of Etiquette, Curtrise Garner

How to Behave, Caroline Tiger

Manners for Moderns, Kathleen Black

My teenage son rolled his eyes and suffered through in great silence. When I was finished reading the titles, I asked: "Is that a real question?" **ONEITA JACKSON**, Detroit, November 2, 2016

Places and Spaces

My first exposure to working was as a child. Saturday nights in the summertime, I was a bartender at an apartment in New York City. There was no pay, but I received profuse praise for my ability to produce a strong drink. Back home, I was on the usher board at church—I even went to usher school. My Mommy taught ushers all over Dayton, Ohio. My paternal aunt moved back from the East Coast in the mid-1980s and opened a restaurant that was deemed too sophisticated for the west side of Dayton; the verbal lashings we received for etiquette breaches were plentiful there. I am 47 years old and I have had a lot of jobs. I worked on Wall Street as a temp. I sold encyclopedias in Ohio and Indiana—well, I *tried* to. I worked at a factory in Dayton, Ohio. I sold hot dogs on a little truck in front of the Office of Management and Budget in Washington, D.C. When I was 18, I wrote bail bond recommendations for Pre-Trial Services. I was a newspaper copy editor 11 years in Detroit. I work at Dr. Faber's dental office around the corner from my apartment building and I work at a restaurant, too. I worked at Budget-Rent-a-Car. I've worked in construction as a project secretary and as a marketing coordinator. I was a concierge at the Discovery Channel Building. I've worked at three universities. I wrote freelance pieces for a major record label. I've helped people apply for citizenship. And more: administrative assistant, secretary, parking lot attendant—I received a 10-cent/hour raise because I was a college student—waitress, ground transportation coordinator, chauffeur, driver, cab driver, office assistant, Spanish-speaking enumerator for the 2000 Cenus, account manager, street concierge, blogger-turned-columnist—I received a 2008 Detroit Free Press Columnist of the Year award—public editor, music reviewer, web editor, data entry clerk, customer service representative, goodwill ambassador, guest lecturer, guest speaker, office manager, Russian translation editor, barback, commentator, fixer, front desk receptionist. Hotel maid, scarf designer, T-shirt designer, street team coordinator. My volunteer work has included answering phones at a public radio station during its pledge drive, helping people learn to read, and feeding people at a soup kitchen. I've been a docent. I've volunteered as a cheerleader at a marathon and I've volunteered at a Baptist church. Today, I tutor kids at a Presbyterian church in my neighborhood. All of these things have presented me with unique and interesting opportunities to interact with and observe people, and to serve them, gladly, too.

Dear Son,

I am writing you this morning because a poem just popped in my head: *Unawares* by Emma A. Lent.

When I was in the fourth grade, we had to learn and recite poems for speech contests. As you know, I won some. In the fourth grade, I won for my recitation of *Guilty or Not Guilty*, whose author is unknown.

I recited Paul Laurence Dunbar poems in perfect dialect, too, winning a contest for my stellar performance of *When Malindy Sings* when I was in the fifth grade.

You know I went to Paul Laurence Dunbar High School and that Dunbar was from Dayton. Your grandfather and uncle graduated from Dunbar, too. I don't know if I ever told you the poet lived in Washington, D.C., in LeDroit Park where we did—remember we used to live across the street from Carver Hall? Dunbar attended Howard University, too, I did not know, and lived just around the corner at 1934 Fourth Street—that's the main street that leads up to the university on the east side of the campus; Georgia Avenue, remember, is the main street to the west.

I channel Paul Laurence Dunbar in *Nappy-Headed Negro Syndrome*. It is the rhythm of Malindy I recall in *Driving Miss O.*

I is deaf.

I is dumb.

I is defiant.

Unawares was someone else's poem. After reciting poems, daily, for weeks, I memorized everyone else's poem.

I remember a girl had the Langston Hughes poem *In the Morning*, and I was disturbed that she didn't recite it right, to my critical expectations. Her cadence was off and she couldn't do the accent right, didn't understand dialect. I helped coach her, but she just couldn't get it.

A few years ago, someone asked me to host a National Poetry Month event at a church—like, good grief, I *hate* poetry. Not because I hate poetry, but because Dr. Woodson taught me too well. I still reference my 1,383-page *New Princeton Encyclopedia of Poetics* from his poetry class and hauled it and about 30 other books with me when I went to the church because *poetry is serious,* I told the people.

Dr. Hudson gave me a *Handbook to Literature* 28 years ago that still informs my writing today. I've since bought two more copies. The *Handbook* keeps my satire honest. I've paper-clipped the "wit and humor" and "satire" entries to ensure my ink pen is doing its job for humanity and that I am representing

Dunbar and Hughes, especially Jesse B. Semple.

Do you know Dunbar and Hughes are on United States postage stamps and that Hughes was influenced by Dunbar? Did you know that Dunbar and the Wright Brothers were friends and that Dunbar edited their newspaper? The Wright Brothers are on a postage stamp, too.

Go, Dayton.

Anyway, I was transported to my childhood when someone at the poetry event got up and recited Hughes' *In the Morning*. Scratch that: The person *read* it. I mouthed the words and cringed as the person butchered the poem. Hughes wrote poems that were not in dialect, I thought, and the unaccomplished reader should have chosen one.

At Howard, many students fancied themselves poets. I did not. I was the sergeant-at-arms in a militant little group called Black Nia FORCE (Freedom Organization for Racial and Cultural Enlightenment). We read a lot and marched and protested and held weekly meetings in 116 Douglass.

Sometimes members wrote and recited poems.

One time I offered to *read* one.

I pulled out my *Black Poets* book from Dr. Woodson's class and read Don L. Lee's *a poem to complement other poems.*

Ovation.

I was so good that my classmate Ras Baraka got up and told everyone he thought that if Haki Madhubuti were there, he would be proud of the way I read his poem. (Lee changed his name. Ras is now the mayor of Newark and his father was the poet Amiri Baraka.)

I was so good that one of the members asked me to read *her* poem. She is now a principal in the Bronx.

As I said, *Unawares* popped into my head this morning as I am considering a piece of writing and headed to church this New Year's Day.

Keep God in your heart, Son, and show His love, let His light be reflected in how you treat others.

Love, Mom

(And get thee to a church!)

January 1, 2017

Letters from Mrs. Grundy

Dear Habibi,

Is it ninety-nine cents or a dollar? Ninety-nine cents, like it says on the sticker? Oh. OK. Thank you.

42.3314°N, 83.0458°W

Dear Mr. Habibi,

May I have my change, please?

44.3148°N, 85.6024°W

Dear Vinny,

"Would you like a napkin?" I beg your pardon, but did you just ask me if I would like a napkin? No, I would not *like* a napkin. You serve pizza, Vinny. I *need* a napkin.

42.3557°N, 82.9972°W

Dear Tonya,

She gave us tea-for-two spoons. We ordered soup. Oh, you *do* have soup spoons? Are these the only two?

42.3317°N, 83.0466°W

Dear D'Antonia,

We ordered soup.

42.3317°N, 83.0466°W

Dear New Kid on the Block,

Work on your icebreakers. "Good morning." "Welcome." "Hello." "How are you?" "Thanks for stopping by." "Hi, I'm Fill-in-the-Blank and this is my place." "Hey, how's it going?" Try one of these before you ask me if I live in the neighborhood. Thus, the frigid stare.

42.3557°N, 82.9972°W

Dear Michelle,

Paul Simon. You. Me. *50 Ways to Leave Your Lover. 50 Ways to Defend Your Barista. 50 Ways to Lose Your Customer.*

42.3557°N, 82.9972°W

One Way to Lose Your Customer

Write a fifty-seven-thousand, two-hundred-thirteen-word defense of your barista without ever using these two: "I'm sorry."

42.3557°N, 82.9972°W

Dear Miss Bertha,

"How much is a chicken wing?" and "Do you take the EBT card?" Two different questions.

42.4340°N, 82.9778°W

Dear Latoquaniysha,

This is the thirty-ninth time you have commented, with alacrity, about the price of my Sunday New York Times. Do you say something to *everyone* who buys the paper?

42.3317°N, 83.0466°W

Dear Mike,

If you don't want cab drivers valet parking at your precious private club, raise your exclusive standards and tell your members to get better friends—or remove the "Valet Parking" sign.

42.3317°N, 83.0466°W

Dear Rhonda,

Look, I'm sorry my hand flew in your face—I am, because my mother did not teach me to do that—she didn't. And I'm sorry I wagged my E.T. Phone Home finger in your face like that white woman did to President Obama. I am. And I'm sorry I yelled at you like I was scolding my child. Loud. Ignoble. Graceless. But—you knew there was a "but" coming, didn't you? What did you expect? How did you think your passenger would react after she cheerfully gets on the bus, pays her fare and greets you, only to be upbraided for standing in the wrong place? And you were new to the route? And you were rude? Moreover, wrong?

42.3557°N, 82.9972°W

Chicken Salad Sandwich

What's your opinion of *Five Easy Pieces*? You know, that one scene ...

34.0928°N, 118.287.°W

Dear Flo,

I'll have a chicken salad sandwich, please, and a water, no ice. Plate. Napkin. Cup. Ice. Miss Flo, may I have a water, no ice, please? Tick tock. Tick tock. Tick tock. Two waters, ice. Miss Flo, may I have a cup, please? Tick tock. Tick tock. And a spoon?

37.0902°N, 95.7129°W

Dear Mary Ann,

I like your green grapes. I gave you the ones I wanted you to weigh and bag. Why did you ask me if I wanted you to put some back?

42.3485°N, 83.0402°W

Dear Meghan,

Yes, I'm aware, au con traire, the customer is not always right. I'm curious, though, about your insatiable need to prove it.

37.0902°N, 95.7129°W

Dear Yusef,

That place where you order the recycled plastic bags—the ones y'all put my carry-out order in? Does it sell utensils? It does? Will you order some, please? You have some, you say? Will you tell that young man at the front to release them, please, on their own recognizance?

42.3557°N, 82.9972°W

Dear Miguel,

We ordered takeout to take out and eat. How do you think we might accomplish this?

42.3557°N, 82.9972°W

Dear Peppermint Patti,

I stand before you today simply seeking a deposit slip. I had not anticipated there would be a redirect to the ATM, where I initially sought solace and said slip. It is my humble desire to return to the ATM to complete this transaction sans servicio de lippo. Therefore, I ask again: "May I have a deposit slip, please?" (Good grief.)

42.3305°N, 83.0670°W

Dear Caitlyn,

I didn't ask for ice cream when I ordered today's special, the peach pancakes à la mode? Oh, I'm sorry, sweetheart, do you know what "à la mode" means?

42.3714°N, 83.4702°W

Dear Lacey,

You are failing to protect the fortress. Didn't you get the tweet? They've been letting us in for a while. Now, step aside.

42.3317°N, 83.0466°W

Great Expectations

"Why would you go to the car wash at 5:52 p.m., O?" *Brandon Cab Driver*

"Because it is open." *Oneita Cab Driver*

42.3305°N, 83.0670°W

Dear Ahmed,

What time does your car wash close? (The sign says 6:00 p.m.) Well, what time do you take your last wash? (The sign doesn't say.) Why don't you put that on the sign, then, instead of yelling at me for trying to support your business during its normal hours of operation?

42.3305°N, 83.0670°W

Dear Malik,

Open those big, bright, beautiful eyes. This is an international hotel and it is not in the hood. Therefore, when someone asks, "Is this the floor where the food is?" understand it is a request for information, a yes-or-no question, not a solicitation of your opinion. "I don't think they have the type of food you're looking for" is no yes-or-no answer. (I might not look Indian, but my mother does.)

42.3321°N, 83.0426°W

Dear Sunshine,

Thank you for informing me that *Queen* is an Indian movie. When I asked for two tickets, it was a desire that you complete a transaction, not an expectation of a movie review. (I might not look Indian, but my Mommy does.) May I have my two tickets, please?

42.4734°N, 83.2219°W

Dear Taylor,

The order was placed 30 minutes ago. You said it'd be ready in 15. I am a famished customer seeking new information and "I don't make the sandwiches" appeaseth me not. Will you sashay your little behind over there and talk to the person who *does* make the sandwiches, please, before a famished customer is overcome?

42.3305°N, 83.0670°W

Dear David,

Thank you for acknowledging me when I walked in and took a seat at the table across from you. I am unsure, however, how to process the information you just gave me, that you have a large party coming in in 30 minutes and it will be a while before I get even a drop of water.

42.3305°N, 83.0670°W

Dear Marcellus,

Make a left right here and another left up there and go straight down that street—we should have *been* at my destination by now. You say you're not going to charge me what's on the meter? I'm not going to pay you what's on the meter, either. I used to be a cab driver, too, man. You say did you read about me in the newspaper? Yes, you *did* read about me in the newspaper. Magazine, too.

42.3305°N, 83.0670°W

Dear Martha,

Let me get all the way inside before you start barking, "It won't go out today." I knew my package wouldn't make your last shipment when I walked in the door five minutes before closing. I was positive you'd tell me it would go out in the morning.

42.3317°N, 83.0466°W

Dear Birgitta,

If you are going to quote your store's return policy—the one printed on the back of the receipt— do it. If you are so compelled to quote your store's return policy to me before you even finish ringing up the sale, then do it verbatim, please.

42.6875°N, 83.2341°W

Return Policy

Returns and exchanges will be gladly accepted at any location within 30 days of purchase. Merchandise must be in saleable condition, have price tags attached, and be accompanied by a receipt. Cash refunds will be made only on cash purchases. All others will be based upon method of payment. All evening-apparel sales are final. No sales adjustments on prior purchases.

42.6875°N, 83.2341°W

Point of No Return

I live in Detroit, Birgitta, and I cannot take the time to drive 34 minutes to return a pair of shoes.

42.6875°N, 83.2341°W

Amortization

Those Yves St. Laurent shoes are still holding up, Birgitta, nine years after I bought them. The receipt has faded, but I can still read the return policy on the back. I can still read the price, too: $280.90.

42.3557°N, 82.9972°W

Dear Chris,

Polish. You and the Boys in the Hood sales team need some. I am growing weary of you space invaders walking up to me asking if I want to buy some weed. Y'all are loud—and I don't mean weed-loud. Discretion, young man. Back in the day, if you wanted weed, you gave a person an inquisitive look. I merely said, "Hello."

42.3557°N, 82.9972°W

Dear Kim,

You are offering free concert tickets to a limited-seating event and demanding that people call your radio show only if they know who the Very Important Artist is? Please.

42.3485°N, 83.0603°W

Merry Christmas

May I see that hat, please? "It's real expensive, O." Is it? "Yeah, girl." May I see it, please—do you have the key to the display case? "Yes." Thank you. Will you wrap this up for my son, please?

42.4351°N, 83.1368°W

The Apology

Am I coming to your New Year's Eve party? Who is this? Who? Oh, hey. No, I'm not coming, but thank you for inviting me. No, my son is flying back from St. Thomas at midnight and I was taking a nap. Oh, no, it's OK. I've been well, thank you. Happy New Year. See you soon.

42.3557°N, 82.9972°W

Forgiveness

Girl, guess who just called and invited me to his New Year's Eve party? Yes. I didn't know who it was because I deleted his number—you 'member the last time I was in there he yelled at me for asking for something that wasn't on the menu? Yeah, it's been months. Let's go by there on the way back from the airport.

42.3557°N, 82.9972°W

Public Service

My smile disarms Miss Delightfully Rude, charmed by my courtesy. (It's not for you, Miss Delightfully Rude, it's for the passengers behind me.)

42.3317°N, 83.0466°W

Familiarity, Contempt

1:15 p.m.

"Miss Jackson?" Yes. "Miss Oneita Jackson?" Yes. "Hi, Miss Jackson. This is Mary (Privanashavaan) calling from Big Bank." Yes. "Miss Jackson?" Yes. "May I call you, 'Oneita'?" No.

42.3557°N, 82.9972°W

212-555-1111

1:22 p.m.

Good afternoon. This is Oneita Jackson calling from Detroit. "Yes, Miss Jackson, what can I do for you?" I just got a call from "Mary" in Sri Lanka. What I want to know is who at Big Bank thought it was a good idea to ask people if you can call them by their first name? "I'll get someone from Mr. Big Bank Executive's Executive Team for you right now, Miss Jackson." Thank you.

1:30 p.m.

We are not friends. My friends call me by my first name. I owe y'all money. Yes, that *is* a concern. You say you can transfer me to someone else?

1:35 p.m.

Yes, ma'am—you say you're going to lower my rate and credit my account? Stellar.

40.7128°N, 74.0059°W

Customer Service

Smile. Think. Excel. Listen. Learn. Acknowledge. Respect.

37.0902°N, 95.7129°W

Dear James and James Etta,

Have you seen that commercial? The one where the announcer says, "Don't waste time going to the post office?" I don't like that commercial because I love going to the post office. And I love stamps. I love stamps the way a woman is supposed to love shoes. My eyes light up when I see the new issues. I'm eager to see what's new. Vibrant colors. New designs. Cool products. (I have a mailbox-shaped bank.) Going to the post office is as exciting for me as going to JFK to pick up my grandmother when I was a child, so it hurts my feelings when I see you rolling your eyes and sucking your teeth and sighing, good grief, when I step to the line with this armload of packages. These are my babies. I've been waiting all day for this hour, for this interaction with you, this final moment with my books. These are my babies. I work hard on them. You see me in here all the time sending them off into the hands of others: *Nappy-Headed Negro Syndrome*. I sign them, draw stick people, write notes, add special touches, and put the people's names in them kinda like stalker letters. My favorite part, though, is affixing the postage stamps, every one. Pull, peel, place. Neatly. Planets. National Parks. Ray Charles. Jimi Hendrix. Paul Newman. Sarah Vaughan. Hearts. Johnny Cash. Flowers. Butterflies. Purple Hearts. 80's. Sometimes I go in my stash.

Thurgood Marshall. Andy Warhol. Marian Anderson. Roy Wilkins. Henry Mancini. Malcolm X. Langston Hughes. I get all giddy picturing how people are going to react after these little packages leave my hands and arrive in theirs. It is a special experience, presenting my babies to the world, waiting to hear how they were received. I cherish this moment. Every trip. Every package. Every stamp. Please don't ruin it for me.

42.3317°N, 83.0466°W

Dear Habibi,

If you call *me* petty for asking for my change, what do you call *you* for assuming you should keep it?

42.3314°N, 83.0458°W

Deipnosophist

Dear Floyd, talk about the weather, ask your customers about their flight, find out how long they're going to be in town, have they traveled to your fair city before? Will they need any restaurant recommendations? You're an airport hotel shuttle driver. Stop giving your passengers advice on how to beat the Breathalyzer.

39.29042°N, 76.6122°W

Dear Rayquond,

An outstretched arm, slightly crooked and raised, is a signal, recognized worldwide, that communicates the idea, "I need a cab. At my feet. Right now." Why are you still sitting across the street?

42.3557°N, 82.9972°W

Dear Mr. Watanabe,

The reason I asked if your lemonade was fresh-squeezed is I didn't see any lemons on the counter and I didn't smell any citrus. The reason I asked where the lemons were is because your sign says, "Fresh Squeezed." The reason I told you to take the sign down is it does not appear to be a fact.

42.6875°N, 83.2341°W

Shoo

Dear Farzaneh, how is it that you needed a translator when I tried to order my food, but you were able to tell me in perfect English that I didn't need a knife when I asked for one?

42.3223°N, 83.1763°W

Dear Kyle,

When you're sitting outside a coffee shop complaining about your new job and having a sonorous discussion about all the idiots who work there and how it could be better, remember this: That "Detroit is like a small town" stuff is true. We all know one another. Though you never said one name, I know the people and place you were yapping about. Sylvia Rector's Restaurant of the Year. Detroit 101. Welcome.

42.3557°N, 82.9972°W

Dear Donesha,

Would I like my change? Bring me my change, please, sweetheart, and I will decide how much to tip you, if at all.

42.3317°N, 82.9778°W

Dear Kenya,

That you checked your reservations and saw none for me does not negate the fact that your hotel shuttle driver has not shown up at the airport for more than an hour. Please.

39.2904°N, 76.6122°W

Dear Habibi,

The place where you order the ninety-nine-cent stickers? Do they have Y2K-type issues? Can they print one-dollar ones?

42.3314°N, 83.0458°W

Dear Bob,

Someone asked me the first thing I'd do if I were elected mayor. I'd convene a meeting of all the Department heads and talk about customer service. Have you done this?

42.3314°N, 83.0458°W

Dear Harriett,

What is your attachment with that there stool that prevents you from rising to assist your customers? Your attachment to that there stool might be the reason we keep walking— out that there door.

42.3485°N, 83.0603°W

Dear Jordan,

You and your little logo-and-insignia team members look right cute standing around chitchatting about Mrs. Grundy types. What would be cuter is if you stop basking in the glow of equivocation and go find out the answer to my question.

42.6875°N, 83.2341°W

Dear Petar,

Look at all the cute little black girls who work for you with their cute little black outfits and their cute ponytails and their cute shapes—it is refreshing to see you place a value on personal grooming and appearance. It's not too cute, however, when I walk over to one counter and the girls sing, in unison, "We not open over here."

42.3485°N, 83.0603°W

Dear Ephraim,

At the other bank branches, there is no see-through casket to pass through for entry and no one hovers around the door at 5:55 p.m. so they can be on time to lock it at 6:00:01.

42.3488°N, 83.0524°W

Dear Marci,

Is court supposed to start at the time it says on my little paper—like, was the bailiff supposed to be out here saying, "All rise!" 30 minutes ago?

42.3314°N, 83.0458°W

Dear Trischelle,

I don't know what you were trying to accomplish by attempting to educate me about the distribution schedule of your magazine vendor—and yes, I have called your store twice in three days—but it was a simple question. It is September 4. Do you have a copy of the September Vogue, yes or no?

42.3488°N, 83.0524°W

Dear Ms. Ghebre,

I intend to purchase this magazine, put it in my backpack, and read it on the plane. The smile I gave to you as I placed it on the counter was your indication to ring it up. The frown you see now is my disgruntlement at your pointing out the price.

39.2904°N, 76.6122°W

Common Cents

This is a newsstand, Ms. Ghebre. If you want to know what is in this magazine and why I am paying eight dollars for it, pick one up and read *The War on Stupid People.*

39.2904°N, 76.6122°W

Dear Bronwyn,

How do you run out of popcorn on Opening Night at the movie theater? *Grand Budapest Hotel* is one of the most anticipated movies of the year—I just dropped off a customer in downtown Detroit and floored it so I could get here on time, only to have to wait in line behind all these people and miss the first few minutes of the movie because you weren't smart enough to keep things popping.

42.4895°N, 83.1446°W

Dear Oneita,

How do you run out of gas—at the airport? With a fare in the car?

42.21629°N, 83.3554°W

Dear Big Mike,

Rayette & 'Nem might demand straws with their wine, but the rest of us don't expect one. If you are going to continue to do that, please do not tell anyone you graduated from bartending school.

42.3314°N, 83.0458°W

Dear Vladimir and Marilyn,

It is appropriate to acknowledge a shopper in your luxury department store, whether that person is in your department or not.

42.6064°N, 83.1498°W

Dear Rob,

Practicing your verb tenses? When we asked for help, yes, we were expecting your assistance right now. Present. We need help now. Not next week. Future. We did not need it yesterday. Past.

42.3485°N, 83.0402°W

Dear Sasha and Svetlana,

You work in a luxury department store. It is appropriate to stop complaining about Management when a shopper is in your area.

42.6064°N, 83.1498°W

Dear Amanda,

You and I are the only people in the gallery. You and I and your phone are the only things in the gallery besides these twenty-seven-thousand-dollar paintings. You and I are the only things that move in the gallery. Notice, I am the only thing moving right now—toward the door.

42.3314°N, 83.0458°W

Dear Peppermint Patti Jr.,

The State of Michigan, the United States Department of State, and this bank have my chicken scratch on file exactly the way I signed the check I just presented for deposit. What hierarchical need are you fulfilling by demanding I sign the check "legibly," to your specifications, thereby committing fraud?

42.3305°N, 83.0670°W

Dear Marvin,

Did you ever see that Washington Post article about the D.C. cab driver who charged the Smithsonian benefactor $92.50 for a ride from over here to over there? *Streets Paved in Gold: D.C. Cabbie Gets $92.* She was too afraid to ask the "formidable man" (read: big black dude) for a receipt for the ride that should have cost $8.40, so she called her people. That was in 1998. Well, I am not some scared little white woman. I'm not "old money New England," not a "widow of a Connecticut aircraft manufacturer." No parvenu, either, like my freshman-English classmate Sean (Puffy) Combs, and I don't have any people. I'm no-money Detroit and I'm going to ask you this just one time, sir: Will you refrain from smoking that cigarette, please, while I am in the back of your cab? Thank you.

42.3305°N, 83.0670°W

R-e-s-p-e-c-t

I used to want to be a cab driver, Marvin. Now that you've put that cigarette out, let me ask you something: What's your opinion of metered rates versus zone fares?

42.3305°N, 83.0670°W

Dear Carolyn,

You have turned a simple transaction into theater of the absurd and I am uncomfortable continuing to stand here and trifle with you. First, you question my purchase, then you place my coin on the table. Now, you're staring at me and it is impolite to stare. Let me break this impasse so I can get out of here: I thought you said the postcard was fifty-two cents. It is? President George Washington's face is on the quarter I did not give you. He would be appalled we are standing here in his mansion and you do not know the value of Susan B. Anthony.

40.8417°N, 73.9394°W

Dear Chip,

Miss Ola Mae would have knocked your teeth out if she had come all the way down here to this hearing, waited for an hour because y'all changed the time, asked you a question, and you stared at her. No home training. But first she would have smacked you for saying, "WHAT?" the first time she asked you if you worked for the Department. My violence flows out on paper.

42.3314°N, 83.0458°W

Dear Beverly,

When I call your Department, why do I have to explain the problem and its ramifications seven different ways, make 93 different phone calls, wait on hold for an average of 72 minutes, and talk to four other people so they can come to the same conclusion as I—that I am making a valid complaint?

42.3314°N, 83.0458°W

Dear Renay and Angela,

Instead of directing your employees to advise me, politely, of course, that my favorite item is no longer on your menu—and hasn't been for months—call your printer.

42.3357°N, 82.9772°W

Polite Dinner Conversation

Dear Darnell, "Choking on my spit." This, as I cut into my lamb meatballs with tomato and roasted red pepper sauce, lemon toasted pine nuts, currants, parsley. Delectable. My mouth was watering, mister bartender. Check, please.

42.3557°N, 82.9972°W

Dear Alvin,

You need to trade that bow tie for a hard hat, because the way you just slid my ink pens out of the way to make room for my plate was like a bulldozer charging at a building, like a steamroller flattening everything in its way. No "Excuse me." No "I beg your pardon." No "May I?" No "Please." No smile. I sign books with those pens—I *signed* books with them after I delivered today's address and when I get home, I'm going to use those same pens to sign the letter of complaint I'm writing about you.

42.3314°N, 83.0458°W

Dear Ameenah,

You should thank me for going across the street and buying three boxes of forks for your restaurant instead of catching a 'tude with me while explaining the reasons you don't have any. I don't care why you don't have any. I simply want to eat my salad; moreover, I do not want any other customer to experience cutlery shock. You're welcome.

42.5145°N, 83.0147°W

Dear Kimberleigh,

You've obviously never been to a black Baptist church. There's this conspicuous thing Church Folk do when they are tipping out and do not want to be noticed: They raise their index finger and creep out as if you can't see them inching along the wall like tortoises. Usually, they are not the only ones scooting out, as this exodus occurs during the epic reading of the Sick List. Now, I noticed you were overwhelmed when I walked into your establishment, but I stood there long enough that you could have made like Sister Mattie Mae McLendon and thrown up that church finger. These two fingers? Peace.

42.3861°N, 82.9119°W

Dear Trayshawn,

When I said, "You need a tissue" and you said, "No, I don't," and I said, "Yes, you do," and you said, "No, I don't," and I said, "Yes. You. Do," I was trying to tell you in a polite way that you had a booger in your nose. All day long, you come out of your little booth and stand over people in their cars. That puts them in a unique position to observe your nasal detritus. Consider *my* position: When someone offers you a tissue, take it.

42.3557°N, 82.9972°W

Dear Kristoff,

You've spent some time in the States, I see. Oh, don't be flattered by this observation. In my country, customer service professionals routinely answer questions you did not ask. I asked how much the hotel's buffet cost. I did not ask your opinion of its value. Now, I'm going to ask you, again, in my best English, "How. Much. Is. The. Lunch. Buf-fay?"

53.5511°N, 9.9937°E

Dear Allison and Jonas and Pedro and Maria and Saad and Bashira and D'Asia'Lanette and Jaquiseion and Piper and Patrick and Rahul and Progga and Michele and Tripp and Terra and Corinne and Chuck and Jon and Frederick and Fredericka and Lauryn and Lauren and Loren and Thomas and Tanika and Jamie and Charlotte and Tol and Keiko and Grant and Grace and Ashley and Theodore and Jameelah and Pierre and Champayne:

Three things: My mother is a 70-year-old black woman from the South. We are both old enough to be your mothers. Neither of us is male. Good afternoon, guys. We *ladies* are doing well.

37.0902°N, 95.7129°W

Dear Patricia,

How considerate of you to escort me to a seat all the way in the front of the room so I can hear better. My proper place today, however, is right there next to your president. It's better if I am facing your group when I deliver this afternoon's address. (You might have noticed I look exactly like the girl your group has been promoting on its website the past few weeks.)

42.3314°N, 83.0458°W

Dear Todd,

I like how you checked all those school kids before they got on the bus today—they are usually raucous and unruly, using crude language like "nigger this" and "nigger that" and "fuck this" and "fuck that." Who at DDOT checks you, though, for doing the same thing?

42.3557°N, 82.9972°W

Thirsty

Dear Rodney, there was no need to text me two times after we spoke, and early in the morning, to find out whether I booked your limousine company for my upcoming Detroit tour. You provided the information I needed the first time we spoke, and I certainly won't be using you now.

42.3557°N, 82.9972°W

Dear Brad,

I did not mean to insult you, but if you've been working for a dealership—managing it—for 17 years, you should know the etymology of the brand of car you represent. For example, the only car I've ever owned is a BMW; my Mommy bought it for me when I moved to Detroit. I know that the car is German and that "BMW" stands for "Bavarian Motor Works."

42.3554°N, 82.9960°W

Dear Beyontsay,

Heard you got fired and I understand why. The fact that you yelled, "Fuck!" while you were at the cash register last week with a line of people out the door, then cursed yourself—"Shit!"—for making yet another mistake, foreshadowed your exit. Where do you go from fuck? To DDOT.

42.3488°N, 83.0254°W

Fare

People stand at the platform because they want to get on the train. They stand at the gate because they want to get on the plane. They stand at the bus stop because they want to get on the bus.

8.7832°S, 34.5085°E; 5405260°N, 105.2551°W; 8.7832°S, 55.4915°W; 34.0479°N, 100.6197°E; 82.8628°S, 135.0000°E; 54.5260°N, 15.2551°E; 25.2744°S, 133.7751°E

Sign Language

Dear Jawana, tell me why you thought I was standing at the bus stop right next to the bus stop sign. Scratch that. Tell me why you rolled right past me standing at the bus stop right next to the bus stop sign. Scratch that. Tell me why you didn't stop at the stop sign next to the bus stop. Scratch that. When you're done with your head-neck-shoulder contortion act, please tell me why you thought I was yelling and banging on the bus.

42.3357°N, 82.9772°W

Dear Shirley,

My son and I were standing at the bus stop today when the driver rolled right past us. There were people standing in the aisles. As the bus rolled by, we could see there were plenty of seats available in the back of the bus. You say he probably didn't know there were seats available? That's the problem.

42.3317°N, 83.0466°W

Dear Wanda,

I look forward to catching your bus every night after I leave work. You are a nice lady and the bus is always on time, plus I get to read my New York Times. This leg brace has been slowing me down, lately, though, and the ice makes walking worse. Did you see me waving my hands or hear me banging on the back of the bus as you rolled by? I had to flag a cab at the Westin to catch you—the next bus doesn't come until midnight. You say you saw me, but you didn't realize it was me?

42.3358°N, 83.0422°W

Dear Leslie and Lamar, Lewis and Lori, Lester and Linda, Lisa and Langston, Lloyd and Lolita, Camille and Calvin, Charles and Charlotte, Corvetta and Corlando, Chester and Charnise, Centrinthia and Centravian,

People stand at the bus stop because they have somewhere to be and they are depending on you to get them there. They cannot afford to miss the bus—or have it miss *them*.

44.3148°N, 85.6024°W

Gift of Time

Dear Marina, I want the purse that's in the window. Oh, it's not for sale—it's a gift with purchase? Well, aren't you in the business of sales? Then ring up the watch and give me the purse and I'll be on my way.

40.7589°N, 73.9851°W

Dear Judith,

Yes, I'm from Detroit, but I am from Uptown, too, and I know this city well. (One time I took a shortcut while I was driving my Uncle J.J. to his job at the post office on 34th Street and someone who didn't know what I was doing started tripping. "Oneita knows New York!" my uncle said. It was kind of like that scene in *Driving Miss Daisy*, where Morgan Freeman takes a different, less circuitous route to the grocery store and Jessica Tandy fusses at him for going the wrong way.)

40.7870°N, 73.9754°W

Dear Marisol and Celia,

I'm always happy to visit your city because your store has no locations in my town. I wanted to apologize, however, for my behavior when your customer, Miss Judith, was in the store. Please forgive me.

40.7870°N, 73.9754°W

Dear Shaun,

Girl, guess what? I had to check this white woman today. I'm at the Swatch store on 72nd and Central Park West, right, and I'm in there being all me—"I'm from Detroit!" and "I just wrote this book!" and doing a photo shoot with *Nappy-Headed Negro Syndrome* and the sales girls are paying me too much attention, right? So this woman—she was Upper West Side, for real—reaches over me and hands one of the girls her credit card. She did not like my enthusiasm, girl, and said, at one point, "This is New York." Like I was some yahoo. That's when I told her I was from Washington Heights. Girl, she was only buying a battery. I took the credit card right outta the girl's hand and handed it back to the woman and guess what I said? I looked at her like she was a child—she was probably 'bout 55, 56—and I said, "Here you go, ma'am. What you're going to do right now is stand there and wait until they are finished taking care of me." I turned back to the girls. She ain't say a word.

38.9072°N, 77.0369°W

Dear Randy,

My friend is very pretty, striking, even, but she's not buying anything today, I am. I have just one more question, please, then you can go back to salivating over her.

42.3485°N, 83.0402°W

Dear Cedric,

This is not Washington, D.C., and I do not live in the White House—although I'd be happy to play Tish Baldrige during the Trump presidency. This is Detroit and I live in an apartment building. For the past 15 years, the simple, quotidian act of leaving my apartment has escaped my notice. Until now. This occasion, as you make it, is not tantamount to a State Dinner and I am not a queen; therefore, it is unnecessary to announce to the entire neighborhood that the "O" is up and out.

Dear French Braid Fred,

The thing about being famous is everyone knows who you are, even if they don't tell you they know who you are, and they are always paying attention to what you do, even when you aren't, especially when you do something stupid, like stand outside an apartment building at 7:37 in the morning bragging to one of your fans about how motherfuckin' famous you are and how niggers be asking you to write them parking tickets and shit, so they can be on TV. Ha ha ha. Heh heh heh. Hee hee hee. The cameras might not have been rolling, sir, but you were being recorded: You are loud as hell and happen to be standing right beneath the window of the chick with the biggest mouth in Detroit. She even referred to herself in the third person in her newspaper column as "Oneita Big Mouth." Now she's writing books.

42.3557°N, 82.9972°W

Encroachment

Dear Lanette, the owner of this bar has just let a 25-piece marching band barge in here and take over the place. They started partying like they were leading a New Orleans funeral procession. Playing like they were at a University of Michigan-Ohio State game. An Army-Navy game. Like they were at a Ticker Tape parade. Like the Detroit Lions had just won the Super Bowl and they were going to Disney World. Like Ed McMahon just showed up to tell them they won the Publishers Clearing House Sweepstakes. Like we were Jamaican and Usain Bolt had just come home from the Olympics. Like they were in the middle of Belle Isle competing with the Marching 100. Like it was 1999 and Jesus had come back for you and for me. It is 2016. I am sitting in a 5,000-square-foot establishment trying to enjoy my food and you think *I'm* being unreasonable for calling the police?

42.3314°N, 83.0458°W

Dear Barbara,

Did you just say, “We have an Arab problem in Detroit”?

38.9227°N, 77.0194°W

Dear Caroline,

That real estate agent y'all hired to take me apartment shopping when I come there? She just told me you have "an Arab problem" in Detroit.

42.3314°N, 83.0458°W

Dear Shaun,

You know I'm leaving D.C. to take a copy editing job at the Detroit Free Press, right? Girl, guess what? The real estate agent they hooked me up with just told me they have "an Arab problem" in Detroit. I said, "Really?" She said, "Yes. We have lots of them. They're everywhere." I kept asking her questions about apartments and then I called the paper. Like. What. The. Bloody. Hell. Yeah, she's picking me up. Wait until she sees MY black behind get off the plane.

38.9072°N, 77.0369°W

Dear Barbara,

Here in the United States, we have a White People Problem. They're everywhere—and they're always saying stupid shit.

38.9227°N, 77.0194°W

Dear Sophia Petrillo,

Picture it: Life with no customers.

34.0928N, 118.3287°W

Dear Erik,

"Suck a dick." I've heard you routinely offend and insult your customers, but please tell me you did not say that to a customer. Please tell me you are not the restaurant owner and you did not say that. Please.

42.3485°N, 83.0402°W

Dear Sanjay,

When I come into your spot for the Tuesday special, I am reminded of my time as a yellow cab driver. When I was a hack—I was a downtown driver—my buddies and I would talk shit about fares and customers. One day I was talking to some neighborhood drivers and I told them when I first started driving in the hood, I was amazed that people were more surprised by the fact that my cab was clean than they were by the fact that I was a woman. Some of them told me that they didn't keep their cabs clean because their customers would get them dirty. I was appalled. "This is *your* workplace," I told them. "Your job should reflect who you are and how you feel about yourself. No wonder no one wants to ride with you." One driver tried to explain, "But we're not like you, O. We're not downtown drivers. We drive in the *hood.*" That word there: Hood. When I come into your chicken spot, I wonder if it would be sparkly, shiny, glistening if it were not in the hood.

42.3488°N, 83.0254°W

Dear Tim,

The young woman who rang up my purchase today is always sweet. She is pleasant and mannerable. Her uniform shirt looks like it spent three weeks in a forest, however, and a fortnight in a Dumpster, followed by a meet-and-greet with baby vomit. I don't know if you've seen her today and I cannot have been the only customer who noticed this and I don't know whether your employees must purchase their shirts from you, but surely someone there must have the authority to slip her another one?

42.3488°N, 83.0254°W

Dear Cleophus,

You're right: I do not go to the Kroger asking for a discount, but this is not Kroger. This is the Heart of Haggling. The farmer who sold you the gladiolus sold out of his and he told me to come get some from you. I did not know you charged more than he, OK?

42.3485°N, 83.0402°W

Dear Patterson,

"What if that's not attainable?" Did you just tell me that a goal I set for my son, an expectation I have of him, is unreasonable? And you're an educator? At a Jesuit high school? In the city of Detroit?

42.4351°N, 83.1368°W

Dear Mommy,

It took great restraint not to smash that white man in his mouth when he said, “What if that’s not attainable?”

39.7589°N, 84.1916°W

Pomp and Circumstance

Dear Patterson, my son will be graduating from a Jesuit university soon.

39.1031°N, 84.5120°W

Dear Marcus,

I was excited when I got on the bus today and learned, through your nonverbal communication, that today's ride was free. I asked you twice, though, after I greeted you, why the bus was free and you just stared ahead. No home training.

42.3557°N, 82.9972°W

Dear Shaun,

Girl, today I got on the DDOT and it was free. Right. I was so excited. But check this out: When I asked the bus driver why the bus was free, he didn't say anything. So, I asked him again, "Why is the bus free today?" Girl, he kept staring down Jefferson. And he wasn't wearing headphones, either. But check this out: I was talking to Lisa about it, right? 'Member I told you native Detroiters have low expectations? Girl, guess what she said? "Why would you ask the bus driver a question?"

38.9072°N, 77.0369°W

Default, Detroit

No.

42.3314°N, 83.0458°W

Yes

"Please." "Thank you." "May I?" "I beg your pardon." "I apologize." "I'll find out." "One moment, please." "Of course." "My pleasure." "Certainly." "With pleasure." "We can." "Yes." "Ladies." "Gentlemen." "How are you today?" "Welcome." "What's going on?" "Yes, ma'am." "Yes, sir." "Good morning." "Good afternoon." "Good evening."

65.2482°N, 60.4621°W; 14.5994°S, 28.6731°W; 33.1376°S, 81.8262°E; 8.7832°S, 124.509°W; 68.4380°S, 160.2340°W

Dear Jacqueline,

I felt welcome when I walked in the door and you greeted me, promptly. I plan to browse your entire store today because I have some new scarf designs in mind and I need some more exquisite yarn; I might even get some more bamboo knitting needles. When I have questions or need assistance, I will find one of you 12 very polite and cheerful ladies. For now, back up, please. Please.

37.0902°N, 95.7129°W

Dear Bruce,

You have some of the best food in Detroit. Everyone loves your shop. We'd love it more if your pococurante employees did not greet us like we walked into a morgue.

42.3485°N, 83.0603°W

Dear Habibi,

In my neighborhood, when the Habibis don't have enough pennies, they give you a nickel, dime, or quarter.

44.3148°N, 85.6024°W

Dear Susan,

I asked you one question. Fact. That question has two answers. Fact. You gave me only one. Fact. Why? Opinion.

38.9566°N, 77.0838°W

Expectations

Dear Susan, my parents taught me to ask questions until I gained some understanding or found out what I wanted to know. I am glad I followed up when you seemed reluctant to give me the full and complete answer to my question: "What credit cards do you take?" (I thought I had enough cash.) You take your store card, the Neiman Marcus card, and I don't have one. To clarify: You also take the Bergdorf Goodman card? Here's mine.

39.7589°N, 84.1916°W

Nonpareil

Dear Susan, one time I was in Bergdorf Goodman dressed as I am today: raggedy jeans, baseball hat, sweatshirt, sneakers. I merely looked in the direction of a dress, and before I could even stare at it in awe, a pulchritudinous sales associate had beamed her Size 2 self over to me and she was standing there, smiling. "Would you like to try that on?" she asked. "Oh, no, thank you," I said, returning her smile. I looked the dress over, planned my exit, and walked out, gracefully. When I was in the hallway, I went straight to the elevator and exhaled—I could not wait to get to the Fifth Floor. That dress cost $30,000!

40.7635°N, 73.9742°W

Oneita Jackson is a satirist who has an English degree from Howard University. The Dayton, Ohio, native spent her summers in Washington Heights, New York City, and she has lived in Washington, D.C., and Albany, New York. Jackson used to make observations as a yellow cab driver and as a newspaper copy editor. Her latest adventure is working as a hostess at Antietam restaurant. She lives in Detroit and is a member of Sonora Missionary Baptist Church.

"I write to save humanity."

ONEITA JACKSON, on people who love to be offended by truth. There is a harsh dose of it in *Nappy-Headed Negro Syndrome*, 13 satires about identity, judgment, and assumptions.

CPSIA information can be obtained
at www.ICGtesting.com
Printed in the USA
FSOW03n0230150217
30679FS

9 780998 647906